Australian Butterflies
Colour and Learn

One of the largest butterflies in the world, the female is bigger than the male and has a wingspan of 16.5 centimetres. When feeding they often flutter their wings and almost appear to be hovering.

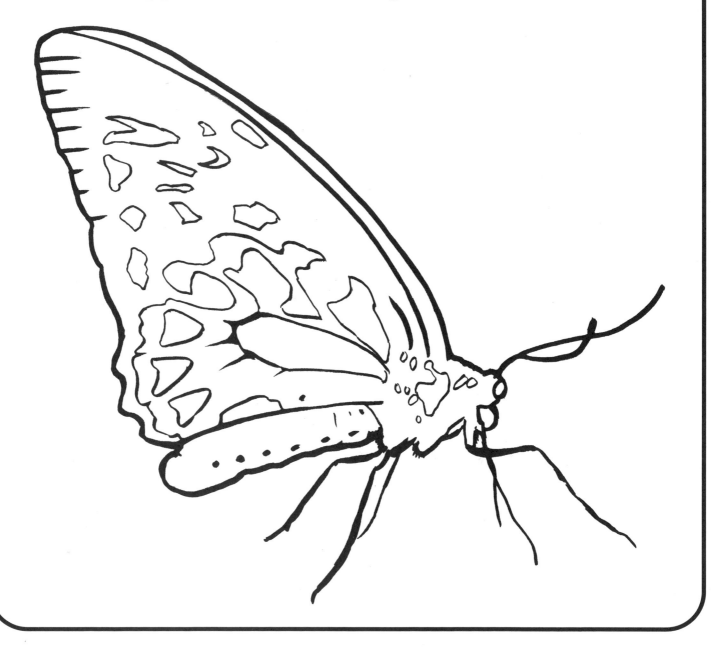

Cairns Birdwing

In suitable conditions this large and attractive-looking butterfly can build up its population and be seen migrating in huge numbers. It can be found right across Australia.

Chequered Swallowtail

Caterpillars of this species feed on native plants such as sandalwood. Sometimes they mistakenly lay their eggs in large numbers on introduced olive trees, which are not suitable as a food plant, so the caterpillars are often relocated by butterfly enthusiasts.

Spotted Jezebel

This species has expanded its range to cover most of Australia thanks to the presence of introduced foodplants from Africa and the Americas. Because the plants they feed on are toxic, the caterpillars themselves become toxic as a defence against predators.

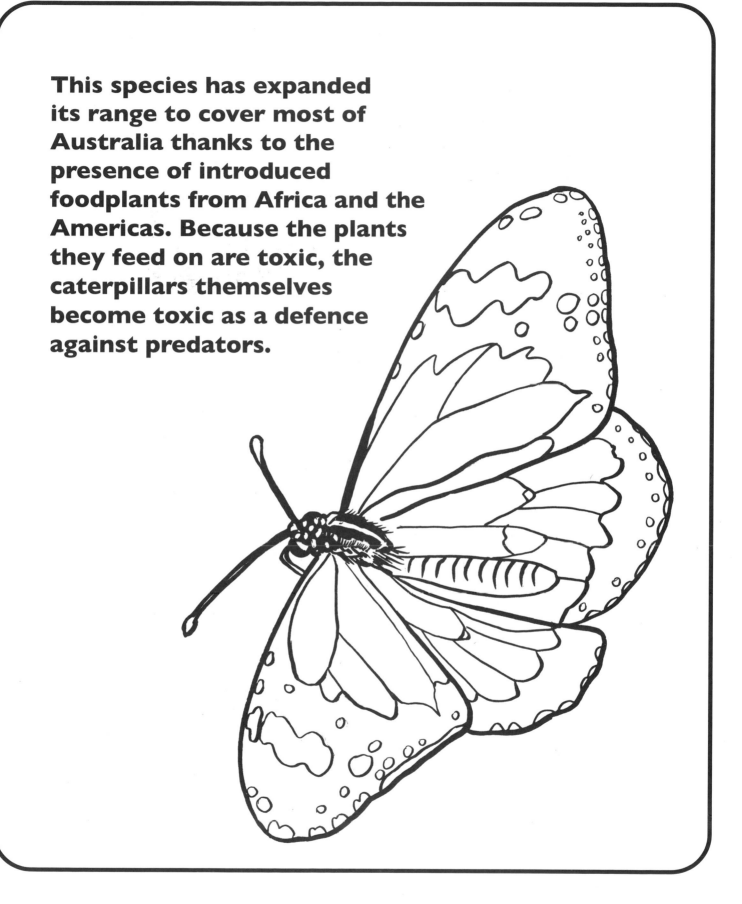

Lesser Wanderer

These beautiful large insects, which have a wingspan of up to 10 centimetres, do not drink nectar like most butterflies. Instead they feed on tree sap oozing from trunks and branches, rotting fruit, animal poo and even the flesh from dead animals.

Tailed Emperor

Familiar across Australia, the Meadow Argus can be seen in grasslands, open woodlands and often gardens. It is thought that the 'eye-spots' on the edges of the wings act as a distraction to draw predators away from the butterfly's body.

Meadow Argus

Occurs widely across the country and the caterpillars will feed on a large variety of different foodplants, including many types of daisies. The adults can travel long distances in large numbers on migration.

Australian Painted Lady

Caterpillars of this species sew together the edges of a stinging nettle leaf to make a shelter for protection. The species occurs widely across Australia. The adults fly fast and can often be seen perched head-down on a wall or tree trunk.

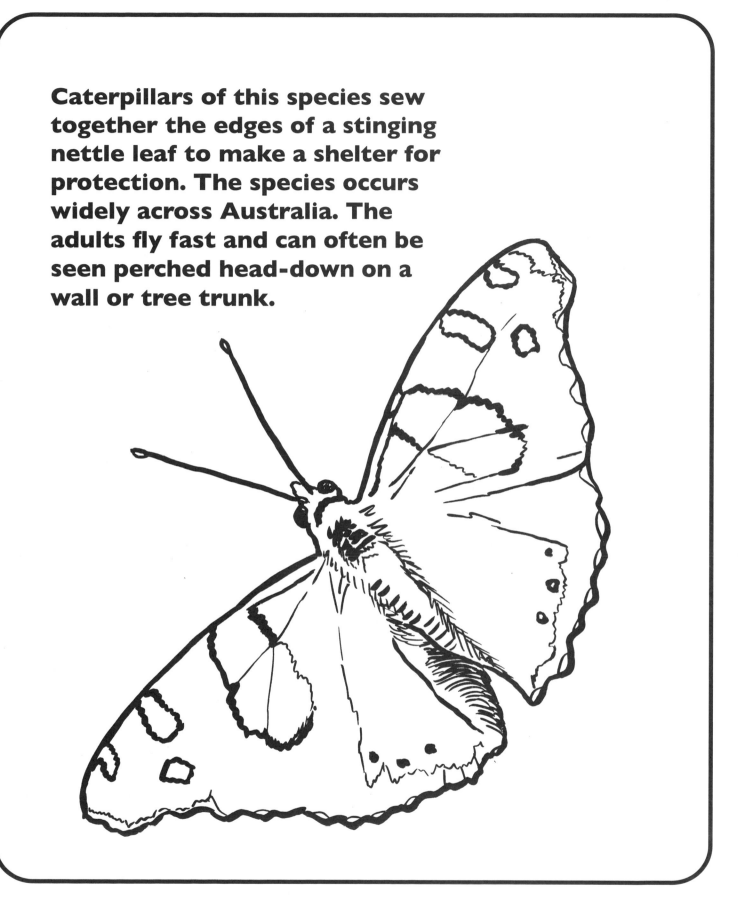

Australian Admiral

This distinctive butterfly has black wings with yellow markings and a striped body with a fiery red tip. It is found only in a few areas along the coast of Queensland and northern New South Wales.

Regent Skipper

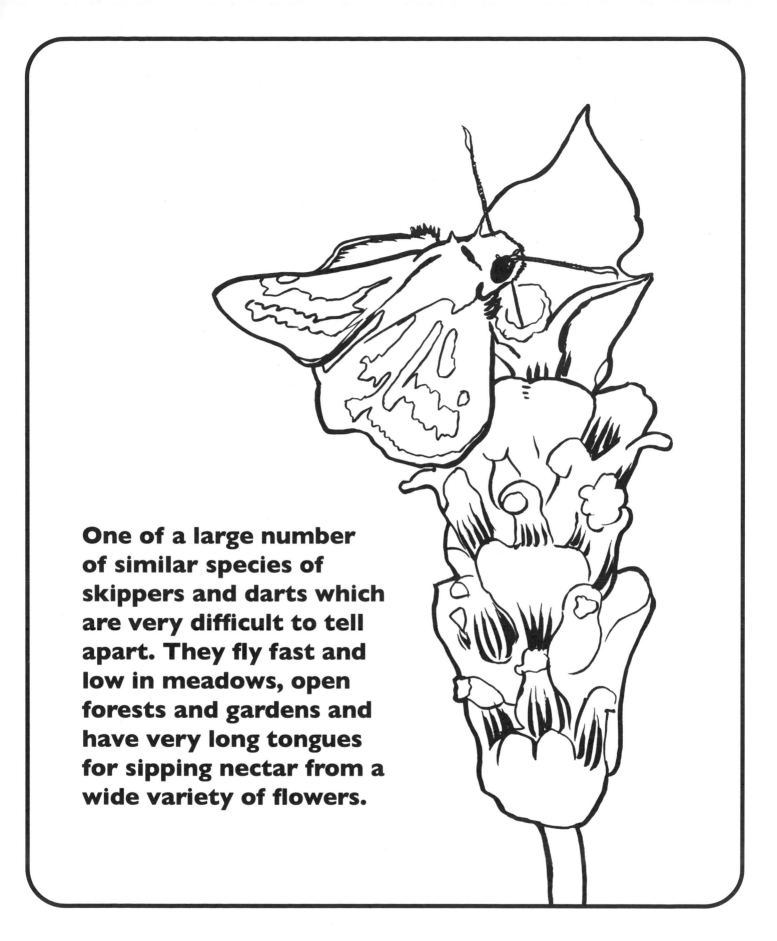

One of a large number of similar species of skippers and darts which are very difficult to tell apart. They fly fast and low in meadows, open forests and gardens and have very long tongues for sipping nectar from a wide variety of flowers.

Walker's Grass Dart

The brilliant blue upperwings are usually closed when this butterfly is resting, so as not to attract the attention of predators. This spectacular species can be seen in rainforests in north and east Queensland.

Ulysses Swallowtail

This small, long-tailed member of the swallowtail family has a wingspan of up to 7 centimetres. It can be found in rainforests in eastern Queensland and north-east New South Wales, and also in Kakadu National Park in Northern Territory.

Four-bar Swordtail

With its eye-catching green patches and habit of spending much of the daytime on the wing rather than perched, this butterfly is very visible in a range of habitats from rainforests to gardens. It is found from north Queensland to Tasmania.

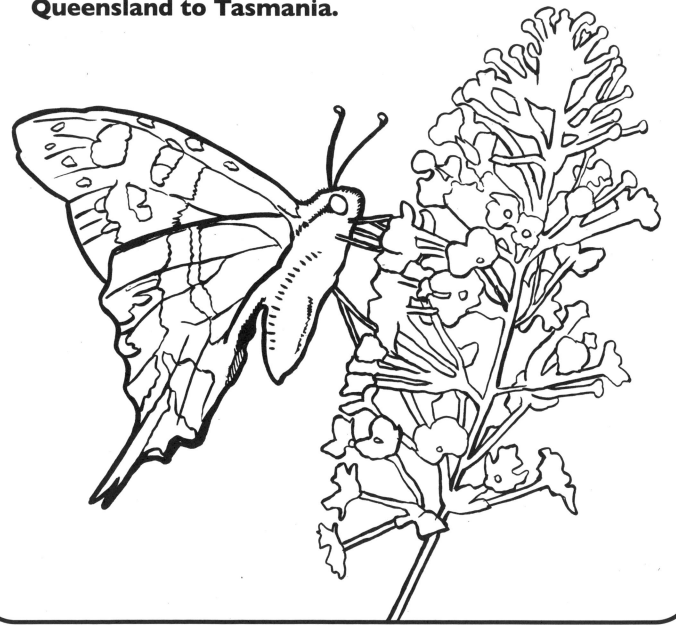

Macleay's Swallowtail

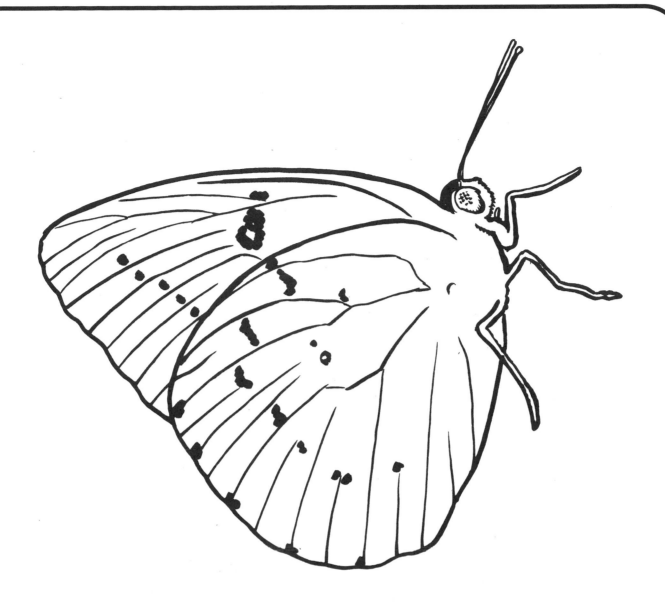

When conditions are right this species can make mass migrations involving millions of individuals. Today these are less frequent in places where its habitat has been destroyed by humans, such as the Brigalow Scrub in Queensland.

Lemon Migrant

Although plain white with black edges on the upperwing, the underwing has an attractive pattern of yellow and black with red and white spots. Found in open woods and gardens in north and east Australia, the caterpillars feed on mistletoe.

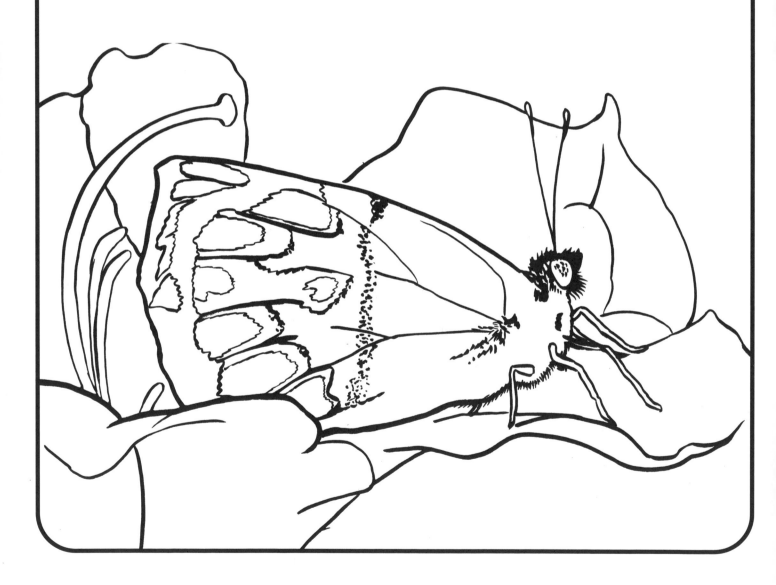

Northern Jezebel

During winter these butterflies migrate to northern Australia and gather together to form large roosts. They breed across northern and eastern Australia and can be found in different types of forests, while they also frequently occur in gardens.

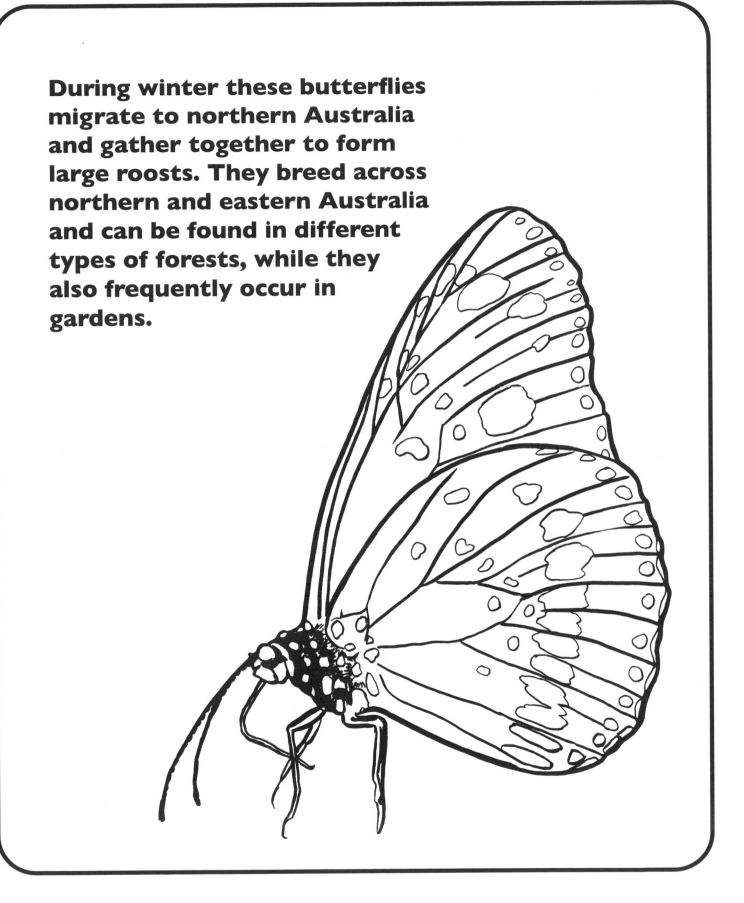

Common Crow

Restricted in range to the Top End within Australia, this beautiful butterfly can be found only in monsoon rainforest and vine thickets in the northern part of Northern Territory.

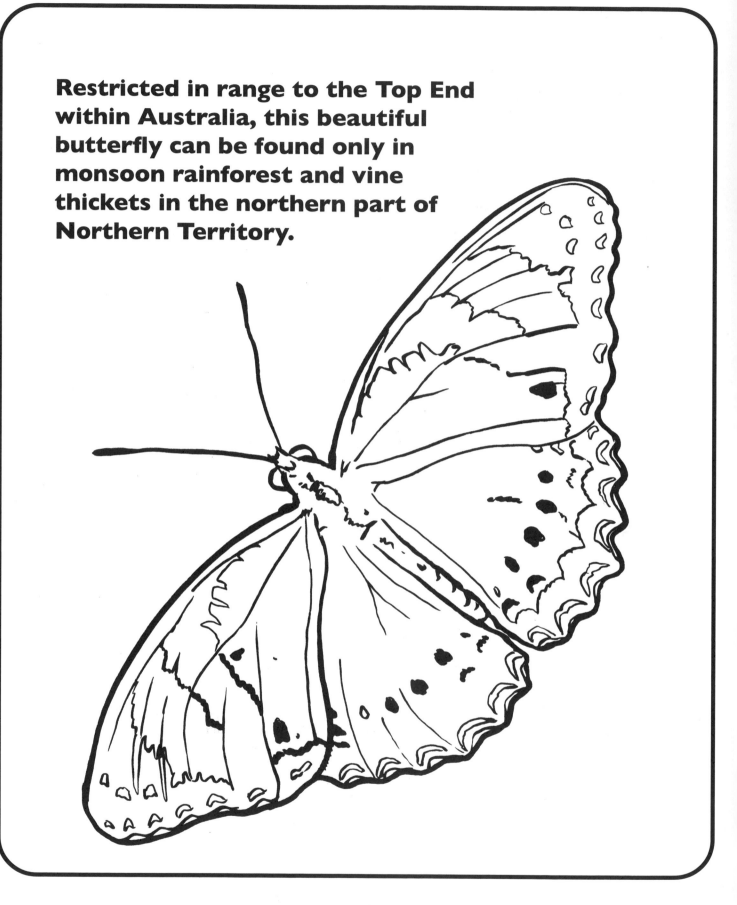

Orange Lacewing

This species is named after the egg-shaped white spots on the male's wings; in New Zealand it is known as the 'Blue Moon Butterfly'. Males are very territorial and will chase away other butterflies and even birds from their patch.

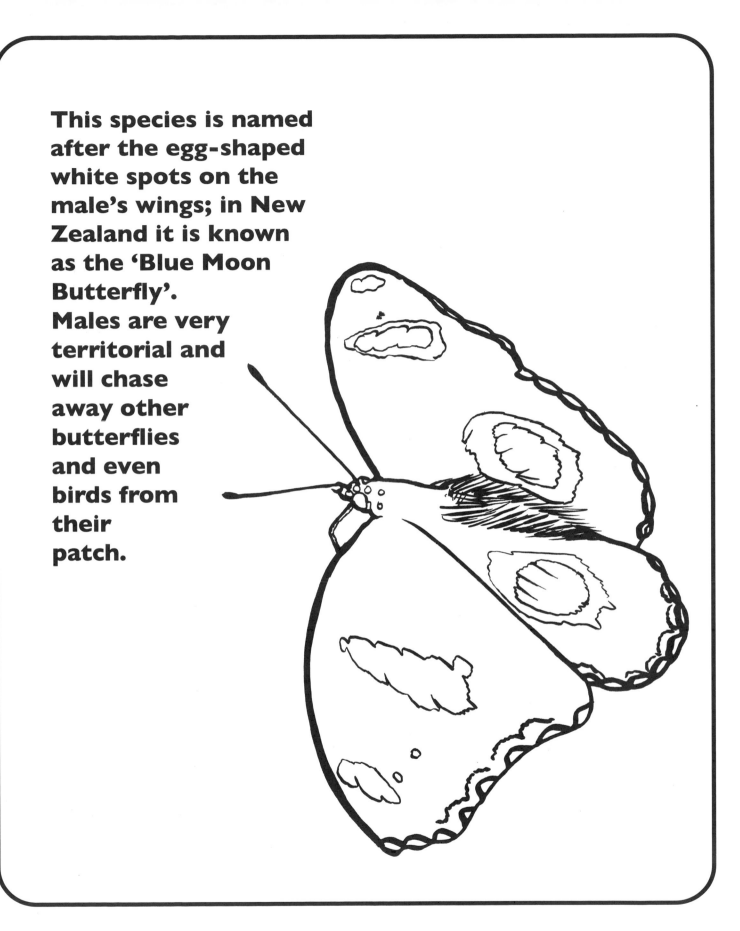

Common Eggfly

One of the most widespread of about 10 species of similar-looking xenica butterflies, the Ringed Xenica occurs widely across eastern and south-eastern Australia and the caterpillars feed on plants such as kangaroo-grass.

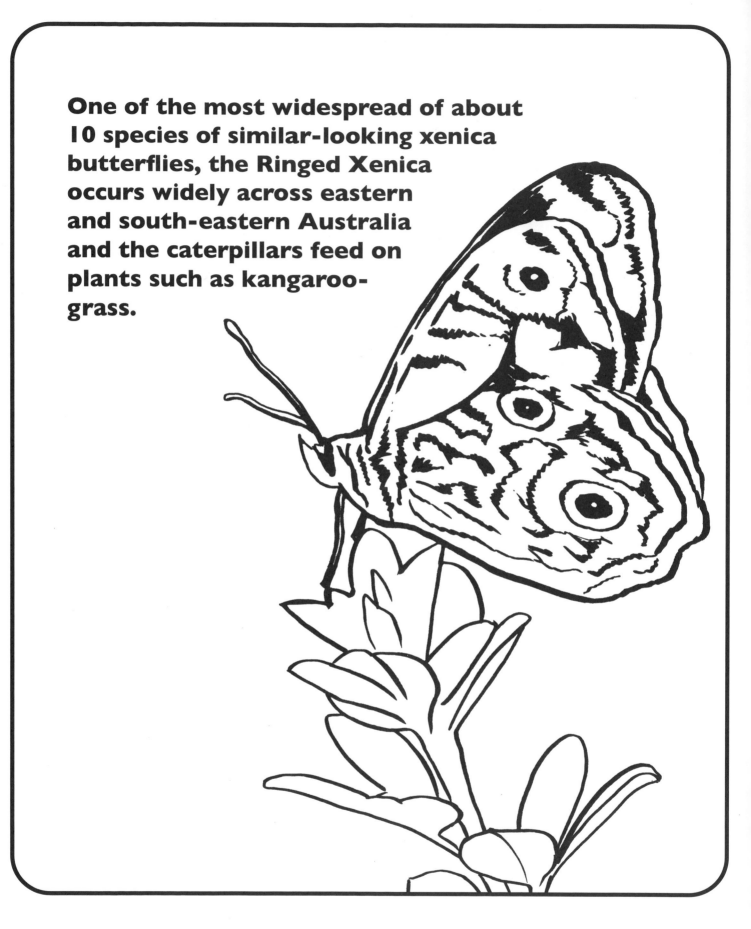

Ringed Xenica

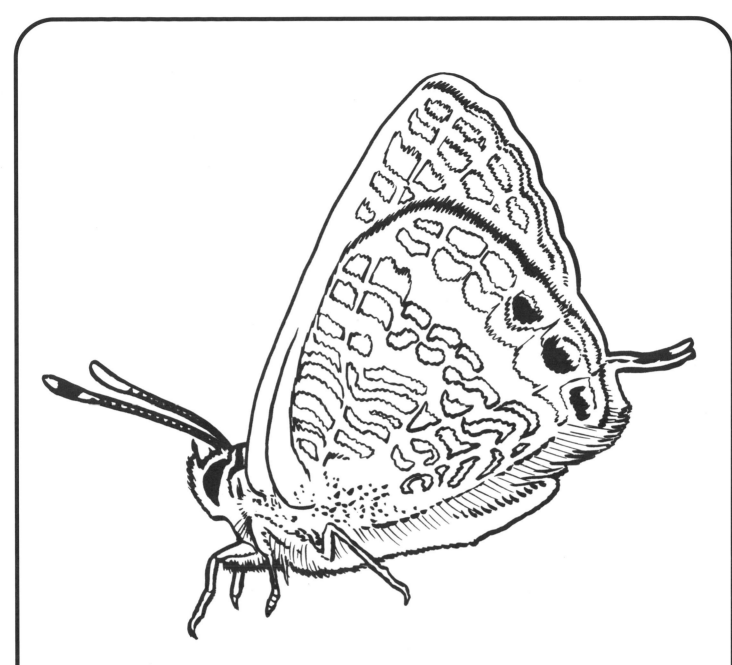

The hindwings of the adults have tiny tail-streamers while the caterpillars feed on pea plants. This is one of the world's most widespread butterfly species, occurring throughout Australia and also across Asia, Africa and Europe.

Long-tailed Pea Blue

This long-distance overseas migrant is a relatively recent arrival in Australia. It became established about 150 years ago, and was only able to do so because its specialist foodplants such as milkweed had been imported and grown by humans.

Wanderer

A specialist of very wet rainforests in north-east Queensland, the beautiful patterns on its wings make this attractive member of the swallowtail family difficult to spot against the green leafy backdrop of the forest.

Green-spotted Triangle

Published in 2022 by Reed New Holland Publishers
Sydney • Auckland

Level 1, 178 Fox Valley Road, Wahroonga, NSW 2076, Australia
5/39 Woodside Avenue, Northcote, Auckland 0627, New Zealand

newhollandpublishers.com

A record of this book is held at the National Library of Australia.

ISBN 978 1 76079 465 1

Managing Director: Fiona Schultz
Publisher and Project Editor: Simon Papps
Designer and illustrator: Andrew Davies
Production Director: Arlene Gippert
Printed in China

10 9 8 7 6 5 4 3 2 1

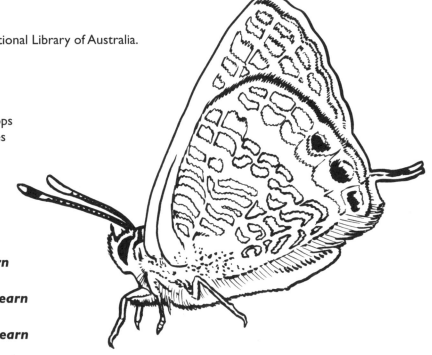

Also available from Reed New Holland:

Australian Birds: Colour and Learn
ISBN 978 1 76079 426 2

Australian Wildlife: Colour and Learn
ISBN 978 1 76079 432 3

Australian Reptiles: Colour and Learn
ISBN 978 1 76079 464 4

Colour With Chris Humfrey's Awesome Australian Animals
ISBN 978 1 76079 424 8

Chris Humfrey's Awesome Australian Animals
ISBN 978 1 92554 670 5

A Field Guide to Butterflies of Australia
ISBN 978 1 92151 788 4

For details of hundreds of other Natural History titles see
newhollandpublishers.com

And keep up with Reed New Holland and New Holland Publishers on Facebook

 ReedNewHolland and NewHollandPublishers

 @newhollandpublishers